SCHOOLS QUALITY ASSESSMENT AND ACCREDITATION (SQAA)

A PRIORITY FOR SCHOOLS

DR DHEERAJ MEHROTRA

Contents

Preface

Ensuring consistent school quality becomes paramount in an age where the educational landscape is in constant flux. The book "Schools Quality Assessment and Accreditation (SQAA)" stems from the understanding that a robust mechanism is required to gauge and enhance the quality of our educational institutions. It provides a roadmap for those who seek to ensure that schools impart knowledge and, more importantly, nurture well-rounded, responsible, and global-minded individuals.

SQAA is not just another educational buzzword; it's necessary in our rapidly evolving world. With numerous educational methodologies, technologies, and pedagogies cropping up around the globe, how do schools measure up? How can they consistently ensure they provide the best for their students? This book attempts to answer these questions, delving deep into the principles, processes, and practices of SQAA.

While the importance of academic rigour cannot be understated, this book posits that true quality goes beyond just academics. It delves into the holistic development of students, the welfare of educators, the involvement of parents, and the school's role in the community at large. Through real-life case studies, practical examples, and expert insights, this book demystifies the SQAA process and showcases its significance in fostering excellence. Furthermore, this book emphasizes the collective responsibility of all stakeholders—teachers, administrators, parents, and students—in the SQAA journey. Everyone has a role to play, and true quality can only be achieved when all parties are active participants in the process. To the educators and school leaders who pick up this book, I sincerely hope you find it enlightening and actionable. May it guide you in your quest for excellence and inspire you to elevate your institution's standards continually. The foundation of a prosperous, enlightened, and harmonious society lies in the heart of quality education. To the future of education, to the future of our children!

Warm Regards,

Dr Dheeraj Mehrotra

www.authordheerajmehrotra.com

ONE

IMPORTANCE OF QUALITY ASSURANCE IN SCHOOLS

"Quality in education is not an act — it is a habit."

The maintenance of quality in educational institutions is of utmost importance for several reasons, each of which contributes to the efficiency of these institutions and ensures that students receive the best education possible. The following is a list of the key factors that highlight the significance of quality assurance in academic institutions:

Improved Educational Outcomes.

The learner is at the centre of the educational experience. Quality assurance aims to ensure that educational practices, syllabi, and resources in schools are optimised to the greatest extent feasible, enabling students to receive the most beneficial education possible.

Stakeholder Confidence:

Parents, guardians, and the community seek reassurance that the school offers a high-quality education to its students. This assurance may be obtained using a rigorous quality assurance methodology.

Ongoing Improvement:

Quality assurance is not limited to upholding specific standards; instead, it focuses on making continuous improvements. It enables educational institutions to identify weaknesses and address them proactively.

Responsibility:

Schools owe a duty of accountability to all of their constituents, but notably to the pupils and their families. Quality assurance methods hold schools responsible for the level of education they provide to their students.

Resource Optimisation:

Schools can ensure that they distribute their resources (both human and material) in the most productive manner by determining what works and what does not within the institution.

Schools that adhere to quality assurance standards and processes may acquire accreditation from recognised authorities, which increases the schools' reputation in the eyes of prospective students, parents, and the community.

Professional Development:

Many quality assurance programs provide instructors with feedback methods, helping them identify areas for improvement in their teaching and professional development.

Schools can ensure that they remain aligned with their purpose, vision, and long-term educational objectives by regularly reviewing and updating their methods and curriculum.

Conformity to Regulatory Standards:

In many parts of the world, adhering to a set of predetermined educational standards is mandatory. The quality assurance process ensures that these requirements are met.

Improved Reputation:

Schools that are well-known for their quality assurance processes are likely to have a higher reputation, making them more appealing to potential students and employees.

Making Informed Decisions:

Quality assurance provides facts and insights that can influence decision-making, from curriculum design to employee hiring procedures.

Holistic Development:

Quality assurance in schools may also focus on other aspects of student development, such as emotional, social, and physical growth, in addition to students' academic achievements.

Ability to Adapt:

The educational environment is constantly evolving, and as a result, new teaching strategies, technologies, and challenges are continually being introduced. The maintenance of quality assurance ensures that educational institutions remain flexible and responsive to these developments.

In conclusion, quality assurance in schools is a comprehensive strategy that employs various methods to ensure that every student has an exceptional educational experience. In a concerted effort to improve academic standards across the board, it fosters collaboration among faculty members, school officials, students, and parents.

TWO

Introduction to SQAA and its Significance

"High-quality education empowers individuals — and strengthens nations."

SQAA, which stands for School Quality Assessment and Accreditation, is an evaluation system designed to preserve and enhance educational excellence in the nation's schools. The School Quality Assurance and Accountability System (SQAA) aims to ensure that schools maintain a specific level of academic excellence by evaluating various aspects of a school's operations. These aspects include the school's curriculum delivery methods, the quality of its teaching, its infrastructure, and the efficiency with which it manages its operations. After being examined, schools are awarded an accreditation status, which is often considered a seal of approval, ensuring the highest possible level of quality.

The Importance of the SQAA

Standardising Educational Quality:

The primary goal of the SQAA is to achieve a consistent level of educational quality across all educational institutions. It ensures that schools of all sizes adhere to academic standards and best practices, regardless of their level of funding.

Continued Improvement:

SQAA is not only about fulfilling standards; rather, it is about establishing a culture that fosters a commitment to continual improvement. It is strongly recommended that educational institutions continually explore new ways to enhance their academic offerings.

Confidence in Stakeholders:

When a school receives accreditation from the SQAA, it inspires confidence in its stakeholders, including parents, students, and the broader community. They may rest easy knowing that the school will provide them with a high-standard education.

Accreditation from the SQAA confers a measure of legitimacy on a school, granting the institution recognition and credibility. This is particularly beneficial for newer or lesser-known organisations seeking to establish their reputation.

Holistic Development:

The SQAA is not just concerned with a student's academic performance. In addition to this, it assesses the schools based on criteria such as extracurricular activities, moral instruction, and the kids' general growth and development.

Optimisation of Resources:

By participating in the SQAA assessment process, schools can identify areas that require additional focus or resources. This facilitates the effective allocation of resources and ensures that no aspect of a school's operation is overlooked during the process.

Feedback and insights gained through SQAA evaluations can also support teachers and administrative personnel in their professional development, helping them identify areas for improvement.

Accountability and Transparency:

The SQAA ensures that schools remain accountable for the performance they deliver. It promotes openness by making it mandatory for schools to be transparent about their operations, strengths, and areas for improvement.

Adapting to Change:

The educational environment is constantly evolving. The School Quality Assurance Act (SQAA) ensures that schools consistently utilise the most current educational techniques, technology, and methods.

Global Compatibility:

A uniform quality assurance system, such as SQAA, guarantees that students graduating from recognised schools are equipped to satisfy international standards. This helps students make a more seamless transition into higher education institutions located worldwide.

In conclusion, SQAA is a crucial organisation in raising the bar for educational quality. It ensures that children receive the best possible education and guarantees that schools will continue to be dedicated to their objective of instilling knowledge, skills, and values in their student body.

THREE

UNDERSTANDING SQAA

"The measure of quality is not what is taught, but what is learned."

Acquiring Knowledge about SQAA (the School Quality Assessment and Accreditation Act)

The increased focus on the quality of education worldwide has led to the development of systems designed to review, accredit, and ensure that educational institutions maintain and uphold exceptional standards. The SQAA is one such program being implemented in the framework of the educational system.

Just what is the SQAA?

The acronym for the School Quality Assessment and Accreditation program is SQAA. It is a systematic method that enables educational institutions to assess their own performance in an all-encompassing, transparent, and exacting way. In this context, accreditation refers to a quality certification awarded to schools after an in-depth review based on a set of predetermined criteria.

Principal Constituents of the SQAA:

Self-review: Before receiving external review, schools must undergo a rigorous process of self-examination to identify their strengths and areas for improvement. This exercise in introspection contributes to the process of establishing standards for the school's overall success.

Evaluation Criteria: The process of determining quality in education is guided by a set of evaluation criteria, which the SQAA defines. These might include, among other things, instructional approaches, curriculum design, student performance, infrastructure, safety measures, teacher qualifications, and community participation.

Review by Peers: Following an internal evaluation, schools often submit their work to external review by their peers. Educators from other schools or professionals in the area will get together to evaluate the institution's adherence to quality standards as a team.

Accreditation: An accreditation status is given once all assessments have been completed and the findings have been collated. This designation is a tribute to the institution's high quality of education and its general efficiency. It often comes with an expiration date, after which a reevaluation is required.

The Importance of the SQAA:

Improving Quality: The SQAA encourages schools to attain and maintain high levels of quality in all areas, from instruction to infrastructure. This helps improve quality.

Stakeholder Trust Accreditation is a signal of trust and assurance regarding the school's quality, serving as a mark of trust for both the community and parents and guardians.

Continuous Improvement: Schools are compelled to consistently improve and innovate in their educational delivery when subjected to periodic assessments and reassessment of their programs.

Benchmarking: The SQAA helps schools benchmark themselves against the most effective educational methods.

Professional Development: The SQAA process's feedback may point the school's administration, teaching personnel, and administrative staff toward areas where they can improve their professional development.

Thorough Evaluation: Unlike irregular and piecemeal assessments, the SQAA provides a comprehensive overview of a school's operation, offering a holistic picture of its strengths and areas for improvement.

The Obstacles and the Criticisms:

Just like any other kind of evaluation, the SQAA is susceptible to the following problems:

Subjectivity refers to the fact that one person's understanding of the criteria may differ, leading to discrepancies.

It Can Be a Drain on Resources: Going through the SQAA process can be a significant drain on resources for many schools, particularly those with limited available resources.

Institutions Could Fight Against Change. Some institutions may resist the change recommended after the SQAA process.

To summarise, the SQAA is an essential instrument for

quality assurance in schools, but for its implementation to be effective, all parties involved need to work together, be transparent, and be committed to the process.

FOUR

THE NEED FOR ACCREDITATION

"Quality education builds not just skills, but character and curiosity."

The Importance of Obtaining Accreditation

Accreditation is a methodical and thorough procedure in which an independent organisation evaluates the quality of a particular institution or program by comparing it to a set of predetermined criteria or standards. Over the course of many decades, it has become increasingly clear that educational institutions, professional training programs, and various other fields require accreditation. The following is a list of the most essential advantages and reasons for pursuing and keeping accreditation:

The Quality Control Process:

An institution or program may be considered accredited if it can demonstrate that it meets the criteria for quality established by an accrediting body.

Ongoing and Continual Improvement:

As part of the accreditation process, institutions must participate in cycles of review, which may include self-evaluation and continuous improvement, thereby cultivating a culture of constant improvement.

Improved Reputation in the Industry:

Acquiring and maintaining accreditation may improve a school's standing with prospective students and their parents, as well as with future employers and the larger community.

Taking Responsibility:

In today's era, when transparency is paramount, accreditation serves as a clear indication that a particular institution or program is meeting the promises it has made and delivering the results it has promised.

Improved Students' Levels of Self-Assurance:

Students can have peace of mind knowing the education they are getting satisfies specific criteria, which may boost their motivation and self-confidence as they continue on their educational path.

Allows for the Smoother Transfer of Credits:

Accreditation makes it simpler for students to transfer their credits across educational institutions, which is particularly helpful for those pursuing further education.

Obtaining Financial Support:
Accreditation is a requirement imposed by a significant number of governmental and non-governmental funding organisations on universities to be eligible for grants, research financing, or financial assistance programs.

Reviews and Comments from Outside Sources:
Accreditation enables schools to undergo an external assessment, providing valuable input and insights that may not be apparent through internal evaluations. This review may be beneficial to the institution.

Making Sure All Practices Are Standardised:
It ensures that institutions maintain standardised procedures across the board, guaranteeing consistency for students regardless of their geographical location or study style. Moreover, it ensures that institutions maintain standardised standards across the board.

Decision-making that Takes Into Account Stakeholder Input:
Accreditation status provides parents, students, and employers with the information necessary to make well-informed judgments about educational institutions and programs.
Stimulates and Promotes Personal Reflection:
The process encourages organisations to reflect on their goal, visions, practices, and results, ultimately leading to a greater awareness of the institution's strengths and areas in which they may improve.
Recognition Around the World:

The capacity of international accrediting organisations to give recognition and comparability worldwide may increase the number of options available to students and institutions operating in global settings. The necessity for certification extends beyond merely fulfilling a predetermined standard; rather, it entails dedication, accountability, and a continued desire to excel in one's field. Accreditation is a vital benchmark and quality marker that ensures institutions remain relevant, influential, and responsible to their stakeholders as the world becomes increasingly interconnected. The demands on education and professional programs expand.

FIVE

The SQAA Process

"Excellence in education demands dedication, not shortcuts."

The SQAA Process stands for "School Quality Assessment and Accreditation."

The School Quality Assessment and Accreditation (SQAA) process is a systematic technique developed to ensure that educational institutions maintain and continually enhance the quality of education they provide to their students. The SQAA process typically involves a set of predetermined standards and criteria against which schools are evaluated. The following is an outline of the process that the SQAA follows, however, the precise procedures may differ based on the accreditation body:

An Evaluation of Oneself:

The institution conducts an exhaustive self-evaluation based on the criteria established by the accrediting entity. This requires collecting data, evidence, and input from various stakeholders, including students, parents, educators, and management. The institution generates a self-assessment report, detailing its action plans and emphasising its strengths and areas for growth.

Remarks Concerning:

The school submits a formal application for accreditation to the accrediting authority, presenting the relevant documents, including the self-assessment report, based on the self-assessment it conducted.

A Brief Introduction:

The accrediting organisation carries out an initial examination of the application and the self-assessment report. Schools may be requested to provide additional data or clarify specific issues after receiving feedback on their applications.

Visit to the Location:

The school receives a visit from an external assessment team or a peer review team selected by the accrediting organisation. The purpose of the visit is to verify the assertions made in the self-assessment report and gain a deeper understanding of how the school operates. During this period, it is not uncommon to have interactions with students, employees, management, and parents.

Report on Evaluations Conducted by Third Parties:

After the visit, the team doing the external evaluation compiles a comprehensive report. This report will provide insights into the school's strengths, areas for improvement, and recommendations. Depending on the methodology the accrediting organisation uses, the report may also contain a score or rating.

Make a choice:

The accrediting body makes a decision on the school's accreditation standing after reviewing the school's own evaluation, as well as those from independent evaluators. Based on how well schools perform in relation to the criteria, accreditation may be granted in one of three ways: full accreditation, provisional accreditation, or denial of certification.

Comments and a Proposed Course of Action:

The input that the school receives from the accrediting organisation is something that it should utilise to make any required modifications and improvements. An action plan may be required to demonstrate how and when the school intends to address the areas of improvement identified during the accrediting process.

Ongoing Monitoring and Accreditation Procedures:

Accreditation is typically awarded for a specified period (for example, five years). After this time period has passed, schools will be required to reapply and go through the SQAA procedure once again. Schools must also uphold the standards they have set for themselves, and they may be subject to interim or periodic monitoring by the accrediting organisation.

Reporting and Openness to the Public:

Many accrediting bodies require institutions to publicly disclose their current accreditation status and the most significant findings from the evaluation. This fosters openness and allows stakeholders to make choices based on accurate information.

The SQAA method is a thorough, systematic, and all-encompassing strategy. Its primary goals are to evaluate and enhance the quality of education in schools. It encourages accountability, ongoing improvement, and the inclusion of stakeholders, ensuring that schools educate their kids with the best feasible education given their circumstances.

SIX

• 24 •
KEY AREAS OF ASSESSMENT

When evaluating schools using a framework such as SQAA (School Quality Evaluation and Accreditation), several key areas of evaluation are crucial in determining the overall quality of the educational environment. One of these areas is the academic achievement of the students.

Collectively, these aspects provide an in-depth analysis of the possibilities, as well as the problems, that the organisation faces in its pursuit of further development.

The following are the most critical aspects of the evaluation:

Positions of Authority and Management:

The efficiency of the leadership and administrative staff of the institution.

The three pillars of strategic planning are vision, mission, and planning.

Participation of stakeholders in the decision-making process.

Management of resources, including financial management and human resource management.

Management of emergencies and standard operating procedures.

Instruction and Student Achievement:

The efficiency and efficacy of the various instructional methods.

The development, administration, and evaluation of educational programs.

Methods and procedures for assessment and evaluation.

Qualifications for teachers, continuing professional development, and regular evaluations of their effectiveness must be in place.

Student engagement and the outcomes of their learning.

Facilities and underlying infrastructure:

Infrastructure includes classrooms, laboratories, libraries, sports facilities, and other amenities.

Access to the use of various forms of technology inside the classroom setting.

Safety and hygiene requirements and recommendations.

Accommodations for pupils who have specific requirements.

Supporting Students and Ensuring Their Progress:

Students receive various support systems, including counselling, career assistance, and remedial programs.

Support for learners from a variety of backgrounds.

Chances within the context of both extracurricular and co-curricular activities.

Progression of students and their achievements in both the academic and extracurricular spheres.

Engagement with the Community and the Outside World:

Participation on the part of parents and of the community at large.

Collaborative efforts with other types of organizations, businesses, or institutions.

Initiatives and activities aimed at providing service to the community.

Mechanisms for input and reactivity to feedback from the outside world.

Morality and principles:

Integrating morality, ethics, and cultural sensitivity education into the school's coursework and extracurricular activities.

The implementation of preventative measures against discrimination, bullying, and other forms of harmful conduct.

Initiatives aimed at fostering civic duty and awareness.

A code of behaviour that applies to students, employees, and other stakeholders.

Ongoing and consistent improvement:

Continual mechanisms for self-evaluation as well as quality control mechanisms.

Adaptability to shifting educational trends, evolving social requirements, and the opinions of many stakeholders.

Methods and activities that are cutting-edge.

Conducting research, developing new best practices, and adapting existing ones.

Management of One's Financial Resources

I'd like you to please ensure that you disclose financial information when requested.

The most efficient use of available resources.

Planning for the long term financially and maintaining sustainability.

Participation of stakeholders in the process of making financial decisions.

Relating to Health and Safety:

Procedures to ensure both the physical and psychological well-being of all involved.

Programs aimed at raising awareness and promoting education about health issues.

Mechanisms for responding to emergencies.

Regularly check your health and take other preventative measures.

Feedback from Stakeholders and Their Level of Satisfaction:

Mechanisms for collecting input from students, parents, staff, and other community members.

Availability to listen to and address complaints and concerns.

A set of actions designed to win the confidence and satisfaction of the stakeholders.

Because each of these critical areas offers a holistic perspective on the school's operations, the evaluation will be comprehensive if considered. The objective is to create an environment that promotes high-quality educational experiences by cultivating excellence in all aspects of school operations.

SEVEN

ROLE OF STAKEHOLDERS IN SQAA

"A school's greatness lies in its students' continuous improvement."

The process of School Quality Assessment and Accreditation (SQAA) involves stakeholders in an essential role. Their participation is crucial because they engage, either directly or indirectly, with the school's ecology, are impacted by the school's policies and practices, and have insights that have the potential to contribute to the school's ongoing development process. The following is a list of the responsibilities that important stakeholders play in SQAA:

Administrative and Leadership Roles in Schools:

Their duty is to ensure that the SQAA requirements are followed wholly and consistently throughout the whole implementation process.

The role is to ensure that the organisation's policies and procedures, as well as its vision and goals, align with the standards, to provide resources for the process, and to lead the organisation's own self-assessment.

Regarding the Faculty and Staff:

Responsibilities include implementing the curriculum on a day-to-day basis, maintaining effective classroom management, and promoting active student participation.

Function: Provide comments on the delivery of the curriculum, teaching techniques, and the setting of the classroom, as well as feedback on areas that might need improvement.

Young people:

Primary benefactors of the educational process are given responsibility for their own learning.

Please participate in feedback sessions and share your thoughts on the effectiveness of teaching, various learning materials, and extracurricular activities. Furthermore, the importance of their academic success and advancement cannot be overstated in this evaluation.

Attention, Parents and Legal Guardians: of contentment, as well as their complaints, are valuable sources of information for the

A parent's or guardian's responsibility is to ensure that their child's educational needs are met in the most effective manner possible.

Comment on matters about school communication, transparency, and safety, as well as the general atmosphere of the learning environment, and their level of evaluation.

Community and Society in the Immediate Area:

The integration of the school within the broader community is the responsibility of the school.

Participate in school events, partnerships, and collaborations, and provide input on the school's social responsibility and outreach efforts. This role requires active participation.

Graduates:

Responsibilities include presenting, in real-world contexts, the results of the educational process undertaken at the school.

The role is to share their perspectives on how the school prepared them for subsequent studies or professions and to identify areas of improvement based on their experiences after leaving the school.

Independent Auditors and the Accrediting Organisation:

Obligation: Ensure that an objective and thorough evaluation of the school is carried out in accordance with SQAA criteria.

In this role, you will be responsible for reviewing the self-assessment report, making on-site visits, interacting with stakeholders, verifying evidence, and delivering a final assessment report along with suggestions.

State and local governments, as well as educational authorities:

In this role, you will be responsible for overseeing the broader educational framework within which schools operate.

In this role, you will be responsible for establishing rules and standards for the SQAA, supervising the accreditation process, and ensuring that schools comply with educational norms established at the national and regional levels.

Partners in the Business and Industrial Sector:

Responsibility: The school is looking for potential employees as well as partners on a variety of different projects.

Participate in skill development activities, provide feedback on the degree to which students are prepared for the labour market, and provide suggestions about areas in which the curriculum should be improved to reflect the requirements of the relevant industries better.

In conclusion, the SQAA process is a collaborative effort that involves various stakeholders, each of whom brings a unique perspective to the table. Their contributions, taken together, guarantee a thorough, accurate, and functional evaluation, which in turn enables schools to attain excellence and maintain a culture of ongoing development.

EIGHT

• 34 •

CHALLENGES IN SQAA

"You can't lift a man by lifting his grade — you lift him by improving his mind."

The School Quality Assessment and Accreditation (SQAA) process is undoubtedly valuable, but it also comes with its fair share of challenges. Recognising these obstacles is the first step in developing successful solutions for overcoming them. The following is a list of some of the most significant challenges encountered during the SQAA process:

Lack of Awareness and Understanding. It is possible that many schools, particularly those in more rural regions, may not wholly understand the SQAA process, its relevance, and its advantages. This may result in resistance or a reluctance to participate in the activity.

Constraints on Resources: The SQAA requires specific standards, which may necessitate the adoption of new technology, modifications to existing infrastructure, and the development of training programs. Certain schools lack the financial or logistical resources to implement such changes.

Established schools that employ time-honoured instructional strategies and business procedures may find it challenging to adapt to the changes recommended by the SQAA process, as they may perceive these recommendations as disruptive.

Varying Expectations from Stakeholders. It may be challenging to successfully manage and harmonise the varying expectations of multiple stakeholders, including students, parents, employees, and the community.

An Abundance of Documentation The SQAA procedure necessitates the creation of extensive documentation. It can be a daunting task for institutions to keep all their records, evidence, and reports up to date.

The entire SQAA procedure, from self-assessment to final certification, can be time-consuming, which may occasionally cause participants to become exhausted.

Training and Capacity Building: The requirement to teach employees and management about the complexities of SQAA may be a challenge, particularly in bigger institutions with high staff numbers. This is especially true for larger institutions.

Maintaining Objectivity: Although self-evaluation is a crucial component of SQAA, it is still possible to be biased. It may be challenging to ensure an assessment that is both objective and open to scrutiny.

Maintaining Continuity and Consistency: After obtaining accreditation, there is a need for ongoing self-evaluation and development to ensure continuity and consistency. It may be challenging to maintain momentum while ensuring standards remain consistent.

Diverse Educational Systems. There are several different boards and curricula that each school adheres to. Aligning these very different systems to a single SQAA standard could provide some difficulties.

Problems Associated with Technology Nowadays, several aspects of the SQAA process can take place online or require digital instruments. This may be particularly challenging for schools that lack the necessary technology infrastructure or expertise.

Differences in culture and setting: a successful strategy for one school in one situation may not be as effective for another school in a different context. The SQAA method needs to have sufficient adaptability to accommodate these disparities, which is already a challenge in itself.

Pressure from outside: Occasionally, there may be pressure from external sources, such as parents, governing authorities, or community leaders, which can impact the SQAA process and the results it produces.

Management of criticism: It is essential for progress to get constructive criticism. Nevertheless, successfully organising, assessing, and acting upon a large quantity of input from various stakeholders may be challenging.

Maintaining Accreditation Once an institution has attained accreditation, the next challenge is to ensure that it continues to adhere to the standards and does not become complacent in doing so. This may be a difficult task.

To overcome these obstacles, the school's administration must take an active role in the problem-solving process, provide ongoing training, organise awareness campaigns, involve stakeholders, and use technology effectively. These obstacles may be efficiently traversed via appropriate preparation and dedication, ensuring the successful implementation of the SQAA process.

NINE

CASE STUDIES

Case Study 1: Conquering a Person's Resistance to Change

The well-known White High School, which has been operating for over three decades, decided to participate in the SQAA process. However, due to the institution's long-standing reputation, several senior faculty and staff members were adamantly opposed to the move. They believed that the institution had already upheld excellent standards.

The challenge lies in overcoming internal opposition to the SQAA process and ensuring that everyone is on board.

The problem was solved when the principal arranged several seminars by outside specialists who elucidated the significance of SQAA and its potential advantages. During the sessions, it was also emphasised how the process might confirm the high standards the school has set for itself rather than merely criticise them. As a result of being aware of the broader picture, the staff's resistance decreased.

Case Study 2 : Managing Resources Within Restricted Capacity

The PAN INDIA Academy, located in a distant community, was interested in becoming an SQAA-accredited institution. Despite this, they were severely limited in resource availability, particularly in infrastructure and technology.

The challenge is to ensure that the SQAA criteria are met while working with minimal resources.

To find a solution, the educational institution worked with local companies and former students to secure sponsorships and contributions. Additionally, they took advantage of various government incentives designed to enhance educational opportunities. They successfully made the required changes to fulfil SQAA requirements by combining their efforts and pooling the available resources.

Case Study 3: Harmonising Various Educational Systems

Background information: Pappu International School adheres to the national curriculum and the International Baccalaureate (IB) program in its teaching methodology. The dual curriculum presented several difficulties in terms of conforming to SQAA criteria.

Integrating multiple educational plans into one that meets the requirements of the SQAA is a challenging task.

A solution was found in forming a special committee that included members with expertise in both educational streams. They devised an all-encompassing structure that managed to keep the most critical aspects of both sets of lessons while also adhering to the SQAA's requirements. This framework eventually evolved into a booklet that served as a guide for all educators.

Case Study No. 4: Keeping Continuity and Consistency in the Workplace

Green Field School has been awarded SQAA certification following its efforts, which have proven fruitful. On the other hand, as time passed, they began to have difficulties upholding the standards.

The difficulty is ensuring that the institution will continue to comply with the SQAA criteria after its accreditation.

A solution was implemented in the form of the school creating an internal SQAA review committee. This group would conduct quarterly evaluations, solicit opinions from stakeholders, and ensure that any deviations from the standards were promptly remedied.

The SQAA process presents schools with various challenges, and each of these case studies illustrates one of those challenges, providing insight into possible solutions. They may act as models for success for other schools just starting on the road to SQAA accreditation.

TEN

• 43 •

THE FUTURE OF SQAA

School Quality Assessment and Accreditation (SQAA) is anticipated to continue evolving to accommodate the shifting educational environment, the integration of technology into educational settings, and the growing importance of quality assurance. The following are some forecasts and trends about the future of the SQAA:

Integration with Computer-Based Instruction:

It is anticipated that the SQAA will develop new methods to evaluate the quality and efficacy of various online learning platforms, online courses, and virtual classrooms as their use becomes more widespread. This will ensure that these digital resources meet the standards that have been established.

Comparisons and Standards on a Global Scale:

As a result of globalisation, there is a growing movement for establishing universal educational standards. The SQAA may work with other international accrediting agencies to develop a set of standards that are more widely acknowledged worldwide. This would make it simpler for students to move between schools in different nations.

The Importance of Continuous Education:

It's possible that the SQAA won't simply concentrate on the standard curriculum in schools, but will also examine how pupils are being prepared for lifelong learning and flexibility in a society that's constantly evolving.

Taking a Holistic Approach:

In the future, the SQAA may place a greater emphasis not just on academic requirements but also on the whole development of pupils. This may include the students' mental health, physical well-being, emotional intelligence, and other areas of development.

Increased Participation from Stakeholders:

In subsequent SQAA procedures, an even greater emphasis may be placed on input from a diverse range of stakeholders, including parents, students, alumni, and community members.

Assessments that are both Continuous and Real-time:

The introduction of continuous, real-time evaluations and feedback might be made possible by recent developments in data analytics and technology. This would enable educational institutions to achieve more rapid progress.

Assessment Standards Tailored to Your Needs:
Because every school has its own set of strengths and weaknesses, there may be a shift toward more individualised evaluation criteria rather than an approach that takes the form of a one-size-fits-all model.

Put More Emphasis on Global Citizenship and Sustainability:
The SQAA may integrate criteria for environmental education, implementing sustainable practices in schools, and developing a feeling of global citizenship in pupils when these issues rise to the status of a worldwide priority.

A Concentration on Educator Continuing Education and Professional Growth:
Future SQAA standards may include a stronger focus on continuing professional development, new teaching approaches, and teacher well-being, given the intimate relationship between education quality and teaching quality.

Combining Machine Learning and AI:
The application of advanced analytics, artificial intelligence, and machine learning can make the accrediting process more data-driven and accurate by analysing patterns, providing actionable insights to schools, and predicting areas that require improvement. In conclusion, the future of SQAA will likely be a growing combination of traditional values and contemporary approaches. This will ensure that schools convey information and nurture creativity, critical thinking, and

overall well-being in the children attending such schools.

ELEVEN

• 48 •

CONCLUSION AND WAY FORWARD

"It is the mark of an educated mind to be able to entertain a thought without accepting it." — Aristotle.

Within the context of the modern educational system, the School Quality Assessment and Accreditation (SQAA) process, which originates in the concept of quality assurance, is of the utmost significance. Schools can assess their strengths and opportunities for growth better, as well as better align themselves with ever-evolving global standards, by engaging in a process that is a complex mix of introspection and external examination.

Insights to Conclude With:

- The field of education is in a perpetual state of transition to accommodate evolving sociocultural, technical, and global norms. This is a need that cannot be avoided. Therefore, the methods for quality assessment, such as SQAA, require ongoing development to remain practical and relevant.
- Approach from a Holistic Perspective: Although academic achievement is still of the utmost importance, the focus has changed to the development of whole people. This is seen by the SQAA's change toward evaluating comprehensive educational experiences, which might include anything from emotional intelligence to sustainability.
- Activated Stakeholders The proactive participation of a wide variety of stakeholders in the SQAA process highlights the collective responsibility involved in forming an education environment that is high in quality.

The Path Forward:

- Embrace Technology: The incorporation of advanced analytics, artificial intelligence, and other new technologies has the potential to make the SQAA process more data-driven, real-time, and predictive. This will enable schools to be proactive rather than reactive.
- Customizable Criteria Considering that every school is different, it is possible that providing some leeway within the SQAA framework may result in a better-tailored and more accurate evaluation.
- Training Sessions and Workshops are conducted regularly. Conducting training sessions and workshops for educators may guarantee that they remain current

with the intricacies and methodology of SQAA, ensuring the proper application of the standard.

- Cooperation and Partnerships: Establishing cooperation with foreign accrediting agencies may give a broader viewpoint, ensuring that our educational institutions align with the best practices found in other parts of the world.
- Feedback system: Ensuring continual development and refinement of the SQAA process may be accomplished via a comprehensive feedback system involving students, parents, and instructors.
- Incorporating Socio-Cultural Aspects. As societies progress, the SQAA should include socio-cultural aspects to ensure that schools maintain relevance in their education approach. This will help shape students into global citizens with a solid awareness of their culture's roots.

Even while SQAA has made considerable advances in ensuring that education is of high quality, the path is not yet complete. The end goal is still to establish a system in which every student has access to an education that is not just of the highest possible standard but also comprehensive, welcoming, and well-prepared for the future. For SQAA to have a prosperous future, the organisation must be open to change, cultivate partnerships, and continue to learn.

TWELVE

ACADEMIC AUDIT PARAMETERS

An Academic Audit is a systematic process of evaluating and improving the teaching-learning ecosystem in schools. Its importance lies in ensuring quality education, accountability, and continuous growth.

The purpose of the Academic Audit is to evaluate the efficiency of the entire academic practices in the school, including teaching, learning, and overall academic practices. To ensure continual improvement, conformity with curriculum requirements, and the development of student outcomes, it serves as an organised instrument.

Assessing the following key areas:

The implementation of the curriculum involves a review of the topic syllabi, lesson plans, and learning outcomes, as well as the incorporation of skills relevant to the 21st century.

Pedagogy, the use of teaching aids, digital integration, inclusion, and student participation are the topics that will be covered in the classroom observations that are part of the teaching and learning practices.

The examination of formative and summative assessment methods, record-keeping, feedback channels, and remedial procedures is included in the assessment and evaluation process.

Verification of teacher qualifications, participation in professional development programs, and attendance at workshops or training sessions are all examples of teacher competency and development responsibilities.

Analysing student accomplishment statistics, involvement in extracurricular activities, assistance to students with special education needs, and career guidance programs are all included in the student performance and support category.

The inspection of the library, labs, information and communication technology facilities, and the availability of instructional resources are included in the infrastructure and resources.

Interacting with students, parents, and staff members to assess their level of satisfaction and collect feedback is an example of stakeholder engagement.

The audit will provide recommendations for building a culture of academic excellence and continual growth, as well as insights into areas of strength and areas for improvement.

References:

https://pt.slideshare.net/dheerajmehrotra/sqaa-by-cbse

https://www.udemy.com/user/dr-dheeraj-mehrotra/

https://www.udemy.com/course/tech-wonders-for-teachers/learn/lecture/19188514#overview

https://www.academia.edu/36150147/Importance_of_QUALITY_in_Schools

https://www.amazon.in/Tools-Quality-Schools-Dheeraj-Mehrotra-ebook/dp/B09QWD3HTK

https://www.youtube.com/watch?v=z9oxrUgxQk4

https://www.booktopia.com.au/academic-quality-management-in-schools-dheeraj-mehrotra/book/9798886843989.html

https://www.kobo.com/in/en/ebook/teachers-favourite-teaching-strategies-that-work

About The Author

Dheeraj Mehrotra, MS, MPhil, PhD (Education Management) H.C.., a white and a yellow belt in SIX SIGMA, a Certified NLP Business Diploma holder, is an Educational Innovator, Author, with expertise in Six Sigma In Education, Academic Audits, Neuro-Linguistic Programming (NLP), Total Quality Management In Education, an Experiential Educator, a CBSE Resource towards School Assessment (SQAA), CCE, JIT, Five S, and KAIZEN. He has authored over 100 books on topics which include Computer Science, AI, Digital Body Language, NLP, Quality Circles, School Management, Classroom Effectiveness and Safety and Security in schools. A former Principal at De Indian Public School, New Delhi, (INDIA), NPS International School, Guwahati, and Education Officer at GEMS, Gurgaon, with ample teaching experience of over Two Decades, he is a certified Trainer for Quality Circles/ TQM in Education and QCI Standards for School Accreditation/ School Audits and Management. He has also been honoured with the President of India's National Teacher Award in 2006 and the Best Science Teacher State Award (By the Ministry of Science and Technology, State of UP), Innovation in Education for his inception of Six Sigma In Education by Education Watch, New Delhi and Education World- Best Teacher Award, BOLT Learner Teacher Award by Air India, 'Innovation in Education Award 2016' by Higher Education Forum (HEF), Gujarat Chapter, among others. He has developed over 150 FREE EDUCATIONAL MOBILE Apps for the Google Play Store exclusively for Teachers, Students, and Parents. This work has been recognised by the LIMCA BOOK OF RECORDS &

INDIA BOOK OF RECORDS as the only Indian to draw that feast. Dr Mehrotra is a PRINCIPAL at KUNWARS GLOBAL SCHOOL, Lucknow, in India. He has conducted over 1000 workshops globally on "Excellence In Education" integrated with Total Quality Management and Six Sigma, Technology Integration in Education (TIE), Developing towards being ROCKSTAR TEACHERS, including Cyberspace, Cyber Security, Classroom Management, School Leadership & Management, and Innovative teaching within classrooms via Mind Maps, NLP and Experiential Learning in Academics. He is an active TEDx speaker and can be viewed on the YouTube TEDx channel.

As a premium UDEMY Instructor, he has developed over 450 courses and caters to over 8 Lakh students from 180 countries.

He can be visited at www.authordheerajmehrotra.com

www.authordheerajmehrotra.com

Scan Here
FOR QUALITY BOOKS
For Home Library for
Parents, Educators &Students